YOUR ECONOMIC FUTURE™

How Interest Rates, Credit Ratings, and Lending Affect You

G. S. Prentzas

ROSEN
PUBLISHING®

New York

Published in 2013 by The Rosen Publishing Group, Inc.
29 East 21st Street, New York, NY 10010

First Edition

Library of Congress Cataloging-in-Publication Data

Prentzas, G.S.
How interest rates, credit ratings, and lending affect you/G.S.
Prentzas.—1st ed.
    p. cm.—(Your economic future)
Includes bibliographical references and index.
ISBN 978-1-4488-8346-2 (library binding)
1. Credit ratings. 2. Interest rates. 3. Loans, Personal. I. Title.
HG3751.5.P74 2013
332.7'43—dc23

                                                        2012014431

Manufactured in the United States of America

CPSIA Compliance Information: Batch #W13YA: For further information, contact Rosen Publishing, New York, New York, at
1-800-237-9932.

Contents

5 **Introduction**

8 **Chapter 1**
Why Credit Matters

17 **Chapter 2**
Understanding Interest
Rates

32 **Chapter 3**
How Loans Work

42 **Chapter 4**
How Interest Rates
Affect You

52 **Chapter 5**
Credit Ratings

59 **Chapter 6**
What's Your Score?

67 **Glossary**
69 **For More Information**
73 **For Further Reading**
75 **Bibliography**
77 **Index**

This couple discusses the terms of a mortgage with a bank's loan officer. Mortgages and other types of credit enable people to make large purchases.

Introduction

Think about an imaginary couple named John and Susan Smith. They find the perfect home for sale for their family. The house is much larger than their current apartment. The house's owners are moving to another state, so they are selling the house at a great price. The children are excited because they'll finally get their own bedrooms. Plus, lots of their friends from school live in the neighborhood.

Like most people, John and Susan don't have enough money to pay cash for such an expensive purchase. To buy the house, they must get a mortgage. A mortgage is a long-term loan used to pay for a house. A bank or other lender gives the borrower money to help pay the cost of the house. The home buyer agrees to repay the loan over time, usually thirty years, with a payment due each month. The loan repayment includes interest, which is a fee charged for borrowing money.

The Smiths go to the bank where they have checking and savings accounts. They fill out a mortgage application. The application asks for information about their jobs, incomes, and savings. It also asks about their debts, such as car payments and credit card balances. The bank requests a credit score for both John and Susan.

Companies called credit reporting agencies keep records of everyone's credit history. Lenders send the agencies information about their customers' accounts and payment histories. The agencies use this information to create a credit history and to assign a credit score for everyone. Lenders use these scores as a factor when deciding whether to approve loans.

Within a few days, John and Susan Smith hear from the bank. There's a problem with their mortgage request. In the past, the Smiths experienced problems paying their bills. Soon after college, John had been in a car accident and had borrowed money to pay his medical bills. Because his first job did not pay well, he did not have much money. He missed some of the loan payments. Susan had also made late payments over the years. Sometimes she paid off other bills instead of sending money to pay off her student loan.

The Smiths also have a high credit card balance. Susan started a new job recently. She used a credit card to buy a new wardrobe. John used a credit card to buy an expensive plasma TV before football season began. They were still paying off the credit card company for these purchases. They had also taken out a five-year loan last year to buy a new car.

The bank's loan officer had good news and bad news for the Smiths. Their credit scores were not very good because of their past payment history and current debts. If the Smiths' scores had been lower, the bank would not have offered them a loan. The bank was willing to approve a mortgage. However, the Smiths did not qualify for a mortgage with the bank's best interest rate. The bank gave that rate only to customers with excellent credit scores. The loan officer offered the Smiths a mortgage with a higher interest rate. Because of this mortgage's higher interest rate, the amount the Smiths would have to repay the bank would be much higher.

The Smiths now faced a dilemma. Should they buy the house, even though the mortgage would cost them more than they expected and perhaps make their finances more difficult in the future, or should they delay their dream of owning a home?

Chapter 1

Why Credit Matters

At the time of this writing, the average price of a new car was more than $28,000, according to research firm J. D. Power and Associates. Imagine having to save up enough money to buy a car. Even if you have plenty of money, you may not want to use a large portion of your savings to make such a big purchase. That's where credit comes in. Credit allows you to buy things in the present and pay for them over time.

The word "credit" comes from *credo*, the Latin word for "I believe." Credit is a promise to repay someone who has lent you money. It is based on a lender's belief that you will fulfill your promise to pay back the loan. To get credit, you must convince a lender that you are trustworthy.

Credit does not increase your income. Using it creates debt. Credit and debt are opposites. Credit is something one person gives to another. Debt is something owed. Usually the something given and owed is money. For example, a car loan is credit for the money a lender gives a person to buy a car.

The person who gives credit is called a creditor. The person who receives credit is called a borrower or debtor.

Credit Cards and Loans

Credit is an important part of modern economies. In the United States, for example, consumer spending makes up about two-thirds of the nation's economic activity. Everything from sales of houses to groceries to payments for the services of plumbers and personal trainers makes up consumer spending.

A significant portion of consumer spending is based on credit. Credit cards and loans are the two major types of credit. Many people pay for goods and services by using credit cards for everyday purchases and taking out loans to pay for very expensive items.

The use of credit helps keep the economy working. It makes smaller sales easier and larger sales possible. Without credit, people would buy fewer goods and services. If businesses sold fewer goods and provided fewer services, they would employ fewer workers. Without credit, business transactions would slow down. National and local economies would shrink.

Credit cards offer consumers the convenience of making purchases without having to pay for them with cash. Credit card companies charge merchants a small fee for each credit card transaction. Despite this cost, many merchants accept credit cards because they offer several benefits. Consumers spend more often when they can use a credit card. Using a credit card allows consumers to take advantage of sales and make unexpected or emergency purchases. Merchants want

Young people are taking advantage of credit cards more and more these days. Using credit cards sensibly is a good way to learn financial responsibility.

to provide their customers the convenience of noncash transactions. Accepting credit cards also makes banking easier for merchants, who don't have to deal with so much cash.

Credit cards also allow customers to buy a merchant's goods on credit without the merchant having to offer credit. The credit card company pays the merchant directly for all purchases made on its cards. The credit card company then bills the credit card holder for the purchases. If the credit card holder does not pay his or her credit card bill, the credit card company must seek to get its money back from the credit card holder. The merchant does not suffer a loss when a credit card customer fails to pay his bill.

Banks and other financial institutions offer loans. Lending money to their customers provides benefits for these businesses. They do not provide credit for free. Lenders charge a fee for the use of their money. When a lender makes a loan, it is unable to use the money until the borrower repays the loan. Lenders want to be paid for losing the use of their money.

Interest

Lending money also involves a risk. Some borrowers will not repay their loans. Even if the customer seems trustworthy, she may get sick or lose her job, making it difficult for her to repay the loan. To get paid for the use of their money and to protect themselves from possible losses, lenders charge interest. Interest is the cost of borrowing money.

Because credit is such an important factor in the nation's economy, the federal government takes action to encourage the availability of credit.

It uses several methods to influence interest rates. Interest rates are the cost of using credit. Low interest rates tend to speed up economic growth. High interest rates tend to slow down economic growth.

In general, the federal government wants interest rates to be moderate. Moderate interest rates ensure a stable economy, high employment, and a growing economy. The federal government also makes sure that creditors and debtors are treated fairly. Congress has passed many laws that protect borrowers and lenders.

Personal Credit

For consumers, credit has many benefits. Using a credit card makes buying things easier. A credit card also provides peace of mind. A credit card enables people to make emergency purchases, such as paying a mechanic when the car breaks down. It also lets people avoid carrying around large amounts of cash. Without credit cards, online shopping would not exist.

Who Needs Credit?

Individuals are not the only ones who need credit. Federal and local governments also borrow money. Governments usually do not take in enough taxes and other revenues for large public projects, such as building bridges or highways. A common way that governments raise money for these expenses is to sell bonds. Bonds are certificates issued by a government that promise periodic interest payments for the life of the bond. For example, an investor buys a ten-year Treasury bond issued by the federal government for $1,000. The U.S. Treasury pays the bondholder interest every six months. The investor receives $1,000 back after ten years. Bonds are, in effect, loans. The government takes the money it makes from selling bonds and uses it for public works. It then repays people who bought the bonds, with interest.

During the construction of houses, contractors often borrow money to pay for bricks and other building materials. Contractors repay the loans once they receive payment for completing construction.

Companies also use credit. They borrow money to expand their businesses, buy new equipment, and buy raw materials to make their products. Some small businesses rely on short-term loans to pay their employees and suppliers. For example, when building a house, a contractor often gets a large portion of the money only when construction is completed. However, the contractor must pay carpenters, plumbers, and the building supplies company during the period when the house is being built. A short-term loan helps the contractor pay workers and suppliers.

Some credit cards offer benefits, such as purchase protection if an item bought with the card is lost, stolen, or damaged. Some credit cards give cash back or other awards, such as airline miles or discounts for purchases from certain merchants. Credit also enables consumers to make large purchases. A person would have to save money for a long time to pay for expensive items, such as houses, cars, and major appliances. Loans enable people to make these important purchases.

To receive credit, a debtor must sign a contract with a creditor. The contract spells out the terms of the credit arrangement. A credit card contract specifies a credit line. A credit line is the maximum amount of money the credit card holder can owe. For example, if a person has a $5,000 credit limit, a $500 purchase may be denied if the person already owns the credit card company $4,800. A loan contract shows the amount of the loan and the interest rate being charged. It also specifies how the loan will be repaid. Many loans require a monthly payment. Credit card and loan contracts also provide details about late fees, legal fees, and other penalties if the debtor fails to make payments on time.

Debt

Most people cannot avoid some level of debt. Few people make enough money to pay for their homes, cars, and college educations. Credit provides many benefits. It can also cause problems if a person amasses too much debt.

Personal financial advisers draw a distinction between good debt and bad debt. Good debts are ones that buy items that increase in value or help the borrower create income in the future. For most people, borrowing to pay for education is an example of a good debt. A college education or career training usually increases a person's future income. Although tuition rates have risen dramatically over the past decade, interest rates on student loans have remained low.

Many college and trade school students take out loans to help pay for their education. Earning a college degree is one of the best investments a young person can make.

Taking out a mortgage to buy a home is usually a good debt. Home prices have traditionally risen over time, making the debt pay off in the long run. Mortgages also have lower interest rates than most other types of loans.

Bad debts usually involve buying items that lose their value or do not help the borrower create future income. Bad debts may also have high interest rates. Credit card debt is the primary example of a bad debt. Credit cards usually have high interest rates and finance fees. If the borrower does not pay his credit card bill in full every month, the interest costs add up quickly. Higher credit costs make the items purchased more expensive.

Payday loans are another type of bad debt. In a payday loan, a borrower writes a personal check to the lender for the amount he wants to borrow, plus a fee. The borrower must pay back the money when he receives his next paycheck. Interest rates for payday loans are extremely high. According to the Federal Trade Commission, they can reach as high as 300 percent. To take advantage of good debt and to avoid bad debt, consumers must take charge of their credit.

Chapter 2

Understanding Interest Rates

Interest is the charge for the use of money. When a person needs a loan to buy a home or a car, the loan includes what is called a finance charge. A loan's finance charge is usually expressed as an interest rate. An interest rate reflects the cost of borrowing money. It also has a major effect on the total cost of a loan.

The prices for credit are mostly determined in the same way that the prices for goods and services are set. The forces of supply and demand are the primary factors that determine the interest rate for loans. Other factors also affect interest rates.

Supply and Demand

Supply refers to how many goods or services manufacturers and suppliers offer at different prices. If the price for a specific product increases, suppliers are willing to produce and sell more of that product. If its price decreases, they will likely produce and offer to sell less of the product.

Demand refers to how much of a product consumers are willing to buy at a specific price. If the price of a product falls, demand usually increases because more consumers are willing to buy the product at the lower price. Also, individual consumers may buy more of the product at the lower price. Likewise, if a product's price increases, demand usually decreases because fewer consumers are willing to pay the higher price for it.

The time of the year can influence the supply and demand for products. For example, the supply of fresh vegetables increases during summer, when they grow. As a result, prices for vegetables tend to be lower during that season. Vegetable sellers lower prices to increase the demand for their perishable products. In winter, the demand for swimsuits and

The interaction of supply and demand influences the price of fruit and other products. The same economic principle applies to the price of loans.

flip-flops decreases because fewer consumers want to buy these items during cold months.

Economists call the point where supply and demand for a product meet equilibrium. At equilibrium, supply is equal to demand. Suppliers are producing the exact number of items that consumers want to buy at that exact price. Supply and demand for most products have an equilibrium supply and equilibrium price.

These two elements can move up or down for a wide variety of reasons. For example, an increase in production costs can raise the price at which a seller is willing to offer its products. An overall drop in consumer spending will decrease demand and, therefore, the amount of goods consumers want to buy.

To understand the basics of supply and demand, imagine a company that makes umbrellas. If it costs the company $4 to make each umbrella, it may be willing to make five thousand umbrellas to sell to stores at $6 each. The stores, in turn, may offer the umbrellas to consumers at $10 each. If the store sells all of its umbrellas quickly, it may order more umbrellas from the manufacturer. The manufacturer may have a low inventory of umbrellas. Because stores are demanding more umbrellas than it has in stock, it may respond by raising the price it sells each umbrella to stores to $8. The store may raise the price of the umbrellas to $13.

The price increase reflects two things. The store had to pay more for the umbrellas, so its costs are higher. It also noticed that its customers quickly bought up all of the store's umbrellas. The store is willing to risk that enough customers will be willing to pay more for an umbrella. If the store sells fewer umbrellas at $13 because of a prolonged dry spell, it may lower the price to $12 or less. The lower price may increase demand because it entices more customers to buy the umbrellas.

Supply and Demand of Credit

The basics of supply and demand also apply to the credit market. If the demand for credit increases, interest rates will rise if the supply of credit remains the same. Lenders will set interest rates higher because they have more customers asking for loans than they need. Borrowers will accept higher interest rates because credit is scarce. If the demand for credit falls, however, interest rates will fall if the supply remains the same. Lenders will lower interest rates to attract more customers. They do not want their money to be idle and not earning money.

When the supply of credit increases, interest rates will drop if the demand for credit remains the same. Lenders will compete to find borrowers, lowering interest rates to attract customers. When the supply of credit decreases, interest rates will rise if the demand for credit remains the same. The lowered availability of credit allows lenders to find borrowers who are willing to pay higher interest rates.

The demand for credit comes mainly from parties who want to buy goods and services now rather than some time in the future. Almost all governments, businesses, and consumers need credit to buy goods and services that they need for current use. They borrow money from a lender and agree to pay interest because of their current needs.

The main source of the supply of credit comes from savings. When people or businesses put money in savings

When a person makes a deposit at a bank, the funds earn interest for the bank's customer, while providing the bank with money to lend to other customers.

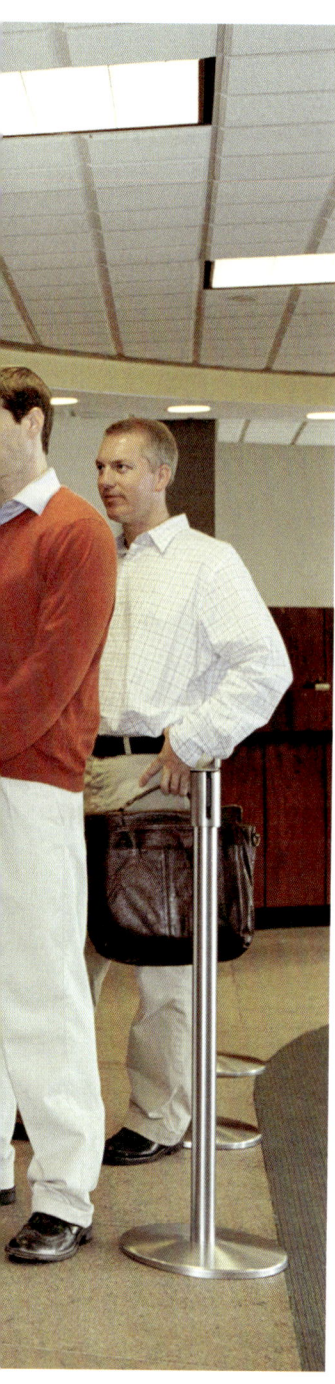

accounts, they are willing to delay spending their money. Insurance premiums, contributions to pension funds and Social Security, and funds in checking accounts are also savings. All of these types of savings are not currently used to purchase goods and services. Savers want to put aside the money so that it will be available to spend in the future.

By bringing savers and borrowers together, banks play an important role in the nation's economy. Banks, credit unions, and other financial institutions pool the savings of their depositors. These financial institutions pay savers interest on their deposits. They then loan the deposited money to borrowers. They make money by charging borrowers a higher interest rate than they pay to depositors. All three parties—savers, borrowers, and financial institutions—benefit from the system.

Other Factors

In addition to supply and demand, several other factors influence interest rates. Overall economic conditions sometimes affect the price of credit.

When a country's economy grows, the demand for credit tends to increase. A strong economy encourages people to spend more because they expect their salaries to rise in the future. More people want loans to buy homes, cars, and other items.

Companies are also willing to take more risks. If business is good, they want to produce more goods, buy new equipment, and hire more employees. However, when a country's economy is shrinking, people and businesses often reduce their spending. Lenders also become worried that borrowers may be less likely to repay loans.

The demand for and supply of credit increases in a growing economy and decreases in a shrinking economy. If the demand for credit increases or decreases by a different amount than the supply of credit, the interest rate will rise or fall.

Inflation also affects interest rates. Inflation is a general rise in prices in an economy. Inflation reduces buying power of money because it causes goods in the future to cost more than they do in the present. In effect, inflation means that a future dollar will be worth less than a current dollar.

Lenders take inflation into account when setting interest rates. A loan involves receiving payment in the future value of money in return for a loan at the current value. Borrowers will be happy to pay back loans with less valuable dollars.

Lenders, however, want to protect the purchasing power of the money they are lending. Lenders will include the expected inflation rate in the interest rates they offer. For example, imagine a lender wants a 4 percent return on its money. If the inflation rate is 2 percent per year, the lender will set the interest rate for a twelve-month loan at 6 percent.

How Inflation Affects You

Imagine that you earn $20 a week for mowing your neighbor's lawn. You like to spend some of your earnings each week by going swimming with friends. The public pool charges $3 for admission. You usually spend $5 at the pool's concession stand. You pay $3 for a slice of pizza and $2 for a soda. After the outing, you still have $12 left ($20 - $8 = $12).

Now imagine that the city raises pool admission to $5 because of inflation. The concession stand also raises its prices. Now pizza slices are $3.50, and a soda costs $2.50. If you go swimming and eat the same snacks, you'll now be paying $11 ($5 + $3.50 + $2.50 = $11). You will have only $9 left ($20 - 11 = $9).

Inflation not only makes things more expensive, it leaves you with less money for other things. If your income stays the same, you must decide to forego swimming, buy fewer snacks, or get by with less money to spend on other things.

The additional 2 percent in interest will compensate the lender for the lower value of the money when the loan is paid back in a year.

Government taxation and spending can also affect interest rates. When the federal government—or a state or local government—spends more than it takes in from taxes and other sources of revenue, it has a budget deficit. It must borrow money to make up the difference. Government borrowing increases the overall demand for credit, which may cause interest rates to rise. When a government spends less than it takes in, it has a budget surplus. A government surplus is a type of savings. Like all savings, a surplus increases the supply of credit, which may cause interest rates to fall.

The Federal Reserve

The Federal Reserve serves as the central bank of the United States. Created by Congress in 1913, it consists of twelve regional Federal Reserve banks. A board of governors manages the organization. The Federal Reserve helps ensure a safe and stable monetary and financial system. It uses its influence on the banking system to keep unemployment low, prices stable, and interest rates moderate.

The Federal Reserve has four main duties. It helps manage the nation's

The Federal Reserve, the central bank of the United States, serves as the place where commercial banks can tap into the nation's money supply.

monetary policy by influencing credit conditions. It supervises and regulates banks and other financial institutions. The Federal Reserve also helps maintain a stable financial system. It provides financial services to the U.S. government, to foreign central banks, and to U.S. banks.

To keep the economy stable, the Federal Reserve increases or decreases the nation's money supply. It does this by buying or selling government securities, such as Treasury bills and Treasury bonds. For example, when the Federal Reserve wants to introduce more money into the banking system, it offers banks holding Treasury bonds an attractive price for the bonds. Selling Treasury bonds to the Federal Reserve gives a bank more money to lend to consumers and businesses.

The Federal Reserve does not directly set the interest rates paid by banks on savings accounts or the interest rates charged by lenders for loans. It does, however, influence interest rates by increasing or decreasing two key banking interest rates.

Federal banking laws require banks to keep a certain amount of money, known as a reserve, in their vaults. Banks need to have money to return to savers who want to withdraw some or all of their money. A reserve ensures that a bank has enough money on hand if many of its depositors ask for their money.

A bank must borrow money when its reserve falls below the required level. This usually occurs when the amount of money a bank lends to borrowers exceeds the amount of non-reserve money it has. The Federal Reserve offers banks short-terms loans so that they can maintain their reserves.

It charges banks a special interest rate, called the discount rate. When the Federal Reserve increases the discount rate for its loans to banks, banks pass along the higher cost to their borrowers. When the Federal Reserve decreases the discount rate, banks can offer borrowers loans with lower interest rates.

The Federal Reserve prefers that banks borrow from other banks rather than directly from it. Loans between banks keep money circulating in the banking system, rather than requiring the Federal Reserve to add more money to the system.

The Federal Reserve sets the interest rate for loans between banks. This rate is known as the federal funds rate or the interbank rate. When the economy begins shrinking, the Federal Reserve lowers the interbank rate, which makes it less expensive for banks to borrow money among themselves. The banks pass these savings onto consumers and businesses.

Interest Rates and the Economy

Lower interest rates encourage consumers and businesses to buy more products and services. They also help stimulate the economy and keep it from sinking into a recession. A recession occurs when consumers are reluctant to spend their money. When consumers buy fewer products, companies struggle to sell their goods. They sometimes lay off workers until consumer demand increases. In turn, unemployed workers spend less because they have less income. The economy spirals downward into a long slump.

Federal Reserve chairman Ben Bernanke delivers a speech in 2011. The Federal Reserve's goal is to keep interest rates at an appropriate level and inflation low.

When the economy is growing, companies are making profits, unemployment is low, and consumers spend lots of money. A risk in a growing economy is that it may grow too fast, which may result in inflation. To help slow down the economy when it is growing too quickly, the Federal Reserve sometimes raises the interbank interest rate. A higher interbank rate results in higher interest rates for consumers and businesses. Borrowers will pay more for credit, reducing their ability to spend their money on other items. Less spending will cool down the economy, making inflation less likely.

Chapter 3

How Loans Work

A loan occurs when one party gives money to another party in return for the promise to repay the money in the future. The repayment of a loan occurs in two parts. The borrower must pay back the amount of the loan, known as the principal. He must also pay the lender a credit fee, known as a finance charge. For example, if a person borrows $100 and agrees to repay $110 in thirty days, the loan's principal is $100, and its finance charge is $10.

Loans provide borrowers a benefit by giving them money to use for a certain period of time. This benefit comes with the obligation to repay the lender. Lenders benefit from loans by earning the finance fee for allowing borrowers to use their money. The amount the lender charges for borrowing the money is usually expressed as an interest rate. The lender's profit from the loan comes with a cost. The lender gives up the ability to spend all or part of the funds for the time period of the loan.

How Checking Accounts Work

In addition to using savings accounts, people can put their unused money into checking accounts. The key benefit of a checking account is that it makes it easier to pay bills. Instead of paying with cash, the account holder can send a check to a creditor for the amount owed. The creditor then deposits the check in its savings or checking account. The business's bank sends the check to the bill payer's bank for payment. The bill payer's bank deducts the amount of the check from his checking account and transfers the money to the creditor's bank. The creditor's bank credits the company's account in the amount of the check.

Banking Basics

Banks and other financial institutions provide savers with a safe place to keep their money. When savers deposit money into savings accounts and certain other types of accounts, their deposits also earn interest. A bank pays its depositors a fee for allowing the bank to use their money. In this case, the bank is the borrower, and the depositor is the lender. A savings account can be a good deal for people who have money they do not want to spend at the moment. Their money is safe in the bank, and it earns them more money. Savers may also be able to withdraw their money anytime they want.

The Federal Deposit Insurance Corporation (FDIC) is the federal agency that insures savings accounts and certain other bank deposits to protect consumers.

Businesses also use the services of banks. They deposit money in savings and checking accounts. They write checks to pay their bills and buy supplies. Although many people still use checks to pay bills, debit cards have become increasingly popular for paying for store purchases. Instead of writing checks, consumers use the debit card to pay for purchases, and the amount of the purchase is deducted from their checking account.

Loans made by banks and other financial institutions enable people to borrow money to buy things that they could not afford if they had to pay in full for them. People often take out loans to buy cars, houses, and other expensive items. Businesses also borrow money from banks to build new factories, purchase new equipment, and pay their employees.

Since banks earn their profits on their loans by charging a fee on the money they lend, they base the interest rate they charge you in part on your credit rating. For most types of loans, lenders require collateral, which is something of value they can claim if the borrower does not repay the debt. For example, when a person borrows money to buy a house, he pledges the house as collateral for the loan. If the borrower fails to make his loan payments, the loan contract allows the lender to take possession of the house. The lender will then sell the house in order to get its money back.

Types of Loans

A mortgage is a special type of loan used for buying a home. Most mortgages have either a fifteen-year or thirty-year term. The borrower must make a payment each month to repay the loan. Each monthly payment includes an interest payment and an amount that goes toward repaying the principal.

In the beginning of most mortgages, each monthly payment consists mostly of interest payments. As the term of the loan progresses, more of each payment goes toward the principal. Eventually, more of a borrower's monthly payment goes to repay the principal rather than to pay interest. As the borrower repays the principal, she builds up an increasing percentage of ownership in the house.

Because a mortgage involves a large amount of money, lenders are more cautious when making

Even a small drop in interest rates to competitive levels, as this advertisement shows, can significantly lower a mortgage's total cost.

loans for homes. They require borrowers to fill out a long loan application. The application requires the borrowers to provide details about their credit and employment history, their current salary, amount of savings and debt, and other personal information. Some lenders are more cautious than others. They will approve a loan only for people who have excellent credit histories and stable employment. People who have credit problems may not be approved for a loan. Even if the lender approves the loan for a borrower with credit problems, the person may have to agree to a mortgage that has a higher interest rate.

People also take out loans to buy a car. Many of these borrowers obtain a loan directly from a bank, credit union, or finance company. Dealership financing is another option. The buyer and the car dealership sign a financing contract. The buyer agrees to pay the amount of money financed, plus the finance charge, over a period of time. Like mortgages, car loans also require borrowers to fill out a loan application. The lender considers the information on the application and checks the borrower's credit score. Dealers sometimes offer lower interest rates on certain models to encourage people to buy their cars.

Student loans are a major financial decision for young people. Like all other loans, student loans must be repaid over time. A student who takes out a loan to pay for education has a legal obligation to pay back the money, even if he doesn't graduate or get a job after graduation.

Students can choose among several different types of student loans. Federal Perkins loans are based on a student's financial need. Although funded by the U.S. government, students apply for these loans through their college's financial aid office. Students repay Perkins loans to the school.

The Federal Stafford Loans Web site (http://www.staffordloan.com) provides information on how the service can help college students borrow money to pay for their education.

Stafford loans are another type of federal government student loan. The Stafford has two different programs, the Direct Loan Program and the Federal Family Education Loan Program. In the Direct Loan Program, students borrow directly from the U.S. Department of Education. They make their loan payments to the Department of Education. In the Federal Family Education Loan program, banks and other private lenders make loans to students. Students repay the lenders. The federal government guarantees the loans. If a student defaults on this type of loan, the Department of Education will pay off the private lender.

Risks and Interest Rates

Although the supply and demand in the credit market determine the general market interest rate, different loans have different interest rates. The characteristics of the borrower and the type of loan involved affect the interest rates for a specific loan. The interest rate for a loan has a major financial impact on a borrower.

All loans involve risks for lenders. A lender considers two main types of risks when deciding how much to charge for providing credit. Lenders evaluate borrowers to determine

Though credit cards allow consumers to make purchases and pay for them later, interest rates can vary considerably depending on the borrower's financial history.

how likely they are to default on, or not pay back, the loan. A lender examines a borrower's history with loans. It asks questions about the borrower's current financial condition. What is the borrower's salary? How long has the borrower held this job? How much debt is the borrower carrying? Lenders must also consider a loan's repayment schedule. A thirty-year mortgage is riskier than a loan with a shorter term, such as a four-year car loan.

The two basic types of interest rates are prime rates and subprime rates. Individual banks set a base interest rate known as a prime rate. The prime rate is usually slightly higher than the current rate for interbank loans. Banks offer their prime rates only to their best customers and to borrowers who have the highest credit ratings. They charge higher interest rates, known as subprime rates, for loans made to customers who have little credit history or a credit history that suggests a greater likelihood of default.

Interest rates can also vary depending on the type of loan. A secured loan will usually have a lower interest rate than an unsecured loan. A secure loan provides the lender greater assurance of getting all or some of its money back in case of default. Unsecured loans will have a higher interest rate because they involve more risk for the lender.

Chapter 4

How Interest Rates Affect You

Interest rates give creditors a reason to lend money. If debtors could not borrow money, they could not pay for homes, cars, and other items. Because credit is essential to many financial transactions, interest rates are an important factor in corporate and personal finances.

Interest rates influence financial decisions made by governments, businesses, and individuals. When interest rates are low, people tend to take out more loans to buy homes and cars. They also refinance existing loans and spend more money on consumer goods. Likewise, businesses obtain loans to build new factories and equipment. In contrast, when interest rates are high, consumers and businesses tend to take out fewer loans. When interest rates rise, credit costs more. Borrowers usually respond to the higher credit costs by buying fewer items using credit.

Interest Rates Matter

Imagine buying a house. The seller accepts your offer of $120,000. You have $20,000 in savings that you want to use for a down payment. To get the rest of the purchase price, you go to a bank and fill out a mortgage application. The bank offers two basic types of mortgages: a fifteen-year mortgage and a thirty-year mortgage. The interest rate they charge will depend on your credit score and other factors. What differences would a higher interest rate and a longer term have on the total cost of your mortgage? Let's take a look at a loan for $100,000:

Interest Rate	Total Cost 30-Year Difference (Term)
4.00%	$171,868
5.00%	$193,252
Difference	$15,384

The difference of 1% translates into a cost of more than $15,000 over the life of the loan.

The Economic Impact of Interest Rates

Interest rates have a major influence on the nation's economy. They affect the housing and job markets and the price of credit. Increases or declines in interest rates can have a significant impact on consumer behavior. When many consumers change their saving and spending habits, it has an impact on local economies and the national economy.

Relatively low interest rates encourage more people to buy homes. Even a small drop in interest rates can have a big impact on the total cost of a mortgage and monthly mortgage payments. Because mortgages are long-term loans, typically lasting either fifteen or thirty years, a lower interest rate can save a home buyer thousands of dollars over the life of the loan. When low interest rates attract more house buyers in a specific area, home prices often rise if the supply of homes for sale is limited.

Likewise, higher interest rates often discourage people from buying homes. A mortgage with a higher rate costs more, making the loan a riskier investment for a family. High interest rates may cause potential house buyers to continue to rent or to buy a less expensive house. The house

Consumers take interest rates into account when making any kind of major financial commitment. Regardless of whether it's a home or a vehicle, the cost of financing can be very high.

may be smaller or located in a less desirable neighborhood. Higher interest rates may also affect the value of a homeowner's house. The lower demand for houses may cause the prices to drop. In some cases, the market value of a house may drop below the amount a homeowner still owes in mortgage payments.

Interest rates also have an effect on the job market. When interest rates are low, companies may borrow more because the risks of investing money in the business are less than when interest rates are higher. With the money from a loan, a business can expand its operations, increase its production, and hire more employees. When interest rates are high, some companies become reluctant to use credit to expand their businesses. High interest rates may even cause companies to reduce the size of their businesses. If consumers are

During the Great Recession, the prices of many homes were forced to drop. The price of homes may drop because of various economic factors, including an increase in interest rates.

using credit less, they may also make fewer purchases. Companies often react to lower sales by laying off employees.

Because interest rates are such an important factor in the U.S. economy, the federal government tries to keep interest rates steady. When the economy is lagging, the Federal Reserve may lower its discount rate or the interbank rate. When the Federal Reserve announces these rate cuts, prices of stocks often go up. Investors expect that banks will offer businesses and consumers lower interest rates. People will buy more goods and services. Companies will ramp up production and create more jobs. If the economy is growing too fast, the Federal Reserve will take action to avoid the risk of inflation. It may increase interest rates to slow down the economy to a more stable rate of growth.

Traders buy and sell shares of companies on the floor of the New York Stock Exchange. When interest rates are low, people may invest in stocks rather than keep their money in savings accounts.

Interest Rates and Personal Finances

Interest rates are important to anyone with a savings account. When you have a savings account, your bank pays interest on the deposits in your account. Banks and other financial institutions need cash to fund the loans they offer. They are willing to pay savers for the use of their money. Interest rates for savings accounts tend to be low. Savings accounts have almost no risk because the federal government insures most accounts.

High interest rates usually encourage people to place more money in savings accounts. They will earn a higher return on their savings. Low interest rates often have the opposite effect. Although money in a savings account creates income, even if the account has a low interest rate, other financial factors have an impact on the interest earned. Federal and state governments tax the interest income most people earn from savings accounts. Inflation also eats away at money in savings accounts. For example, if a savings account earns only 2 percent interest and the inflation rate is 3 percent per year, the money in a savings account loses 1 percent of its value in a year. A low interest rate gives people an incentive to move their money out of savings accounts.

Instead of tying money up in a low-earning savings account, some savers will spend the money. They often invest in stocks or bonds. Stocks are a share in ownership of a company. Stocks and bonds sometimes produce higher earnings than savings account. However, they are riskier investments because the price of a company's stock may fall or the bond issuer may be unable to pay a bond holder for a variety of reasons.

Interest rates are vitally important to someone who needs credit. The cost of borrowing money is based on the interest rate of a loan or other type of credit. A high interest rate results in a loan that is more expensive to repay. The borrower has to use more of his future money to repay the lender. If his income does not grow at a higher rate than the interest rate being paid, the borrower will have less future money to spend. A low interest rate results in a loan that is less expensive to repay. A low interest rate encourages borrowing because borrowers are more confident that they will be able to repay the loan because its total cost is lower.

Chapter 5

Credit Ratings

When a person applies for a mortgage, how does a bank decide whether it should make the loan? How does a credit card company decide whether to give a person a credit card? Credit ratings, or scores, help lenders determine which applicants are good credit risks. An applicant's credit score also affects the interest rates for loans and credit card balances. Some employers use credit ratings when deciding whether to hire a person. Some landlords check credit scores before agreeing to rent their properties. Credits scores show how a person has managed credit and debt in the past. They are an important factor in everyone's personal finances.

Credit reporting agencies are companies that collect information from lenders about their credit customers. These companies are also known as credit bureaus. Equifax, Experian, and TransUnion are the three major credit reporting agencies. They use the credit information they gather to build a credit history for everyone who uses credit. A credit history includes a wide variety of information. For example, it shows the loans a person has taken out and whether the person has paid credit card bills on time.

FICO Score

The credit reporting agencies and other companies use a person's credit history to create a credit rating. The Fair Isaac Company created the first credit rating systems in the 1970s. Its ratings became known as the FICO score. (FICO is a short form of Fair Isaac Company.) In 2006, Equifax, Experian, and TransUnion introduced a rival credit rating system called VantageScore. A credit score gives lenders a sense of the risk of extending credit to a potential borrower.

FICO uses the data from each credit reporting agency to create a person's credit score. The three different credit reporting agencies do not have the exact same data for each individual, so FICO gives each person three different scores. The three scores usually are very close.

The exact formula FICO uses to calculate scores is a secret. However, the company has revealed the five categories that add up to a FICO score. For most people, each category accounts for a specific percentage of their FICO scores.

Payment history accounts for 35 percent of a person's FICO Score. A person's credit history includes information on credit card and loan payments. The key payment history factors that affect a FICO score are the number of late payments, how late a payment was made, and how much money is past due. Late payments on loans or credit card bills usually

Building a Credit History

A young person who has no credit history can build a good credit history. One of the best ways to start a credit history is to open a credit card account. With a traditional credit card, charge only small amounts. Pay the entire balance of your monthly bill on time. If you do not qualify for a regular credit card, apply for a secured credit card. Unlike a traditional credit card, a secured card requires you to give the credit card company a deposit of money. When you buy things using a secured credit card, the company deducts the charges from your deposit. A credit card company will report your card account and your payment history to the credit reporting agencies. Your credit history will start to grow.

There are disadvantages to having a credit card as well. If you miss payments, your credit history will not get off to a good start. Also, credit cards make it easy to fall into debt. There are many financial experts who argue that the risks of having a credit card outweigh the rewards, so be sure to do your research before considering applying for one. Most important, discuss it with your parents or guardian before signing any contract.

lower a FICO score. A person who has paid debts and bills late is more of a credit risk.

The amount of credit a person uses makes up 30 percent of a FICO score. A credit history includes how many credit accounts a person has. It also shows how much money the person owes on each account. Credit card use is a major factor in this category. Spending close to a card's credit limit or having a high credit card balance each month usually lowers FICO scores. This behavior may mean that the person is not handling debt responsibly.

The length of a person's credit history accounts for 15 percent of a FICO score. A person's credit history improves as he or she builds up a longer credit history. How long each credit account remains open also has a small effect on credit scores.

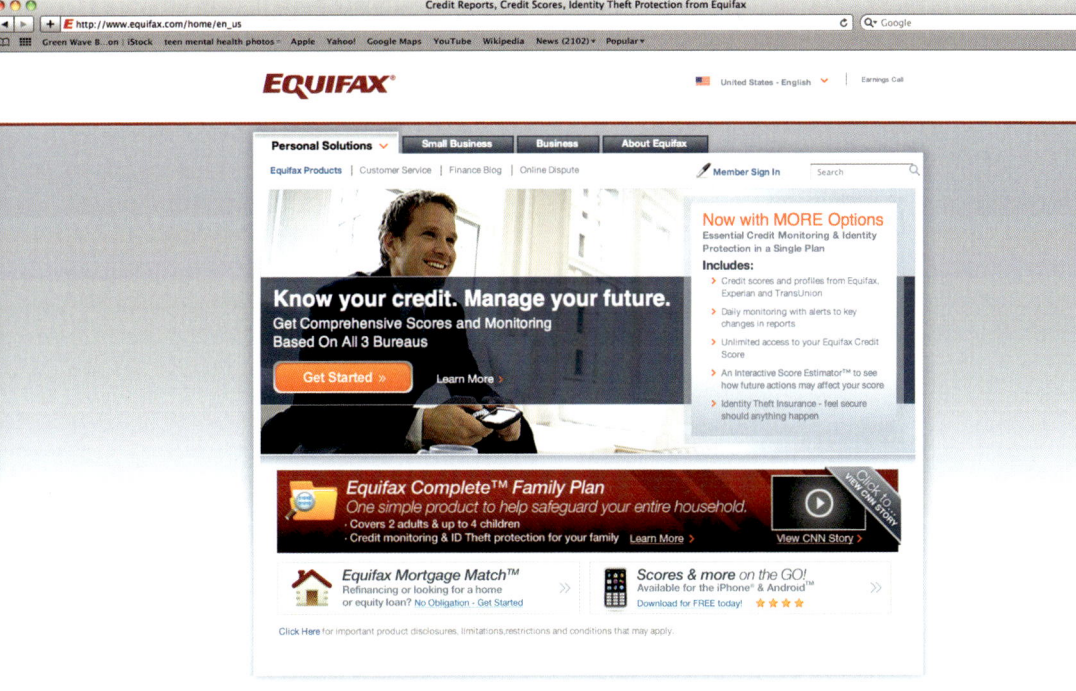

Equifax (http://www.equifax.com), one of the three major credit bureaus in the United States, allows consumers to check their credit scores for a fee.

New credit makes up 10 percent of FICO scores. This data group includes the number of credit accounts a person has opened within the past twelve to twenty-four months. When a person applies for a loan or a new credit card, the lender or credit card company will request a FICO score. Frequent credit requests may lower a score. This part of the score also takes into account recent payments. People who have experienced payment problems in the past may increase their FICO score by making all of their recent credit payments on time.

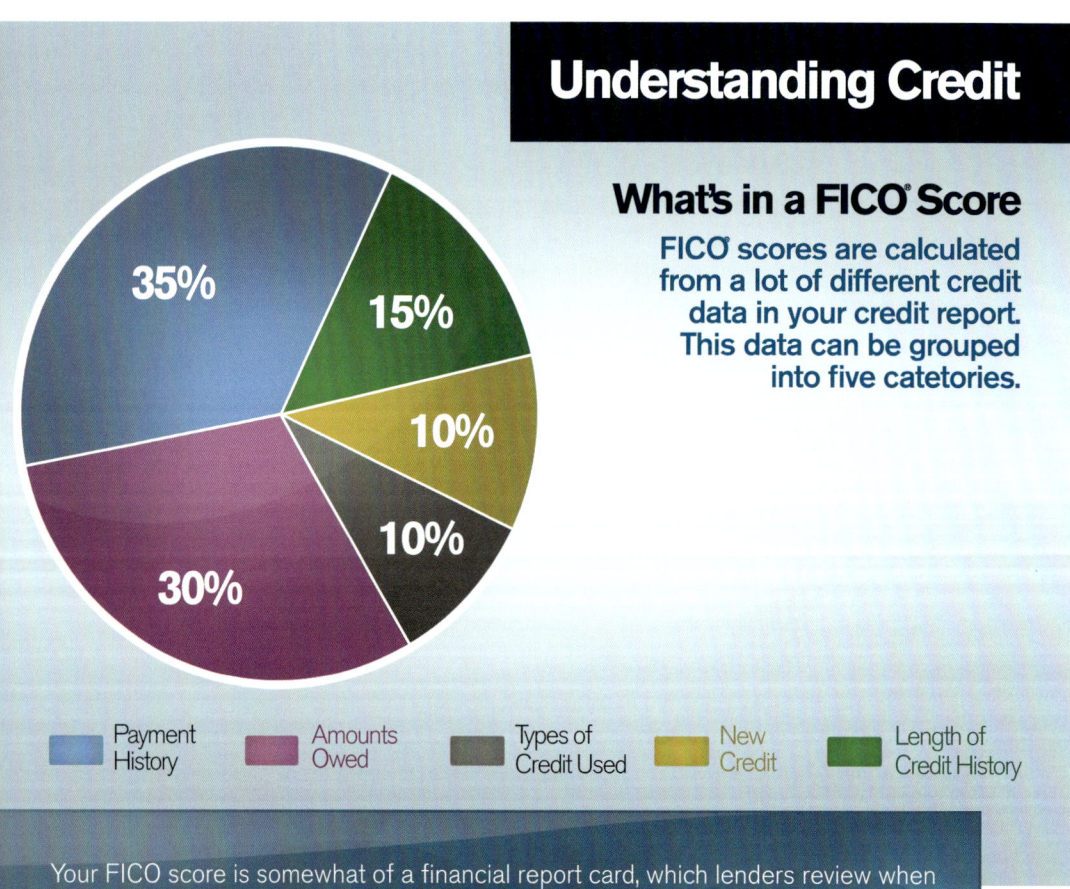

Understanding Credit

What's in a FICO® Score

FICO® scores are calculated from a lot of different credit data in your credit report. This data can be grouped into five catetories.

35%
15%
10%
10%
30%

Payment History
Amounts Owed
Types of Credit Used
New Credit
Length of Credit History

Your FICO score is somewhat of a financial report card, which lenders review when determining what interest rate to charge you.

The types of credit that a person uses makes up 10 percent of a FICO score. There are three basic types of credit: installment loans, consumer finance loans, and revolving credit. Using different types of credit will improve a person's FICO score.

A FICO score takes into account only the information in a person's credit history. It does not include other details about a person. Age, race, color, gender, national origin, or marital status are not part of a FICO score. It also excludes a person's occupation, employer, and salary. However, some lenders look at issues other than FICO scores when deciding whether to approve a loan. They may consider an applicant's income, employment history, and other factors. Federal law prohibits lenders from using age, race, color, gender, or national origin in making lending decisions.

A FICO score is a three-digit number. The highest score possible is 850, and the lowest is 300. A higher score means that the person is more likely to repay a loan on time based on financial history.

The scores are sometimes divided into five levels. People who score in the highest level (775–850) have excellent credit histories. People with scores in the next level (675–774) have very good credit histories. In most cases, lenders will approve credit for people with FICO scores in these two groups. The people in the middle level have average FICO scores (625–774). They are likely to be approved for credit, but they may have to pay slightly higher interest rates than borrowers in the two highest groups. People with below average FICO scores (500–625) may have a harder time qualifying for credit. They may qualify only for subprime loans, which have significantly higher interest rates than standard loans. The lowest FICO scores (300–500) indicate a poor credit history. People with scores in this range are unlikely to qualify for a mortgage or many other types of credit. Lenders will offer them only subprime loans.

VantageScore

The three major credit bureaus have their own credit scoring system, called VantageScore. It is an alternative to FICO. VantageScore differs from FICO in several ways. The score is based mostly on data collected over the past two years. The scores range from 501 to 990. It uses letter grades to measure a person's credit health: A (901–990), B (801–900), C (701–800), D (601–700), and F (501–600). VantageScore also predicts future scores for borrowers. These scores help lenders make credit decisions about people with short credit histories.

A VantageScore credit report costs less than a FICO credit report. Many lenders who do not need a credit score based on a long history find it a better choice than FICO. Companies that lend large amounts of money, such as mortgage lenders, still rely on FICO scores. They provide a more accurate summary of a person's entire credit history.

Chapter 6

What's Your Score?

Before credit scoring, getting a loan or credit card application approved often involved a very long wait. Lenders had to gather information on loan applicants from many sources. Lenders and others who use a person's credit history to make decisions can now get credit reports fast. This speeds up loan approvals, rental approvals, and employment background checks.

Credit scores allow retailers, Internet sites, and other businesses to offer instant credit. These businesses can set a specific credit score requirement. If a customer's score equals or exceeds this score, the person qualifies for credit automatically.

Credit Scores and Loans

Lenders use credit scores when deciding whether to risk giving their customers credit. For many lenders, a person's credit score is the major factor in a loan or credit card approval. A high credit score enables a person to qualify for almost all types of credit. A person with an average score may experience occasional credit application rejections. A person with a poor score will likely encounter difficulties when trying to get a loan or a credit card.

If shopping for a new car, keep in mind that your credit score can affect the interest you pay for a car loan.

Perhaps the most significant impact of a person's credit score is the interest rate paid for the credit. People with excellent credit histories can qualify for a lender's best interest rate. Those with blemishes in their credit history may have to pay higher interest rates. The impact of interest rates is particularly important for large loans, such as mortgages and car loans. Even a slightly higher interest rate can make a loan much more expensive.

Other Effects

Lenders are not the only parties who use credit histories. Some employers conduct background checks on job candidates. A background check will verify the information a candidate provided on the application. It may alert an employer to any concerns about the employee.

A background check will include information on education, job history, and criminal record. It may also include a person's credit history. A potential employee's credit history may indicate the person's reliability and trustworthiness.

Employers sometimes check the credit histories of applicants before making a hiring decision. This helps them determine whether the applicant is reliable and trustworthy.

An employer must get the potential employee's consent before requesting an employment credit report from one of the credit agencies. Employment credit reports do not contain the same information as credit reports sent to lenders. Like credit reports, they provide information about credit and payment history. However, they may also contain information about arrests, bankruptcies, and lawsuits.

Employment credit reports do not include a credit score. The credit reporting agencies and human resources experts agree that a credit score has no relation to job performance.

Fair Credit Reporting Act

Congress passed the Fair Credit Reporting Act to make sure that credit reporting agencies provide credit histories that are complete and correct. Everyone with a credit history has the right to receive a copy of his or her credit report.

Consumers may contest the accuracy or completeness of information in their reports. They must file a dispute with the credit reporting agency and with the party that supplied the information to the bureau. The agency and the party will investigate the consumer's complaint and correct any incorrect information. The consumer can add a summary explanation to a credit report if the dispute is not resolved to his or her satisfaction.

A high or low score may mislead employers about a candidate's fitness for the job. Thus, employers see only a list of the candidate's credit accounts and the person's payment history.

Some landlords also request credit scores before renting apartments or other properties to tenants. A housing credit report includes a credit score and a record of any previous evictions. A low credit score may provide a landlord with a legal reason to not rent to you. Even if the landlord agrees to the rental, the low score may encourage him or her to require a higher security deposit. Landlords typically ask for an advance payment equal to either one or two months of rent. This security deposit protects them in case a tenant stops paying rent or damages the property.

Establishing a Good Credit Score

Because so much depends on a person's credit history and score, personal financial advisers recommend that consumers avoid behavior that can tarnish their financial reputation. Past payment history is a major factor in credit scores, so consumers should pay bills on time. Consistently paying bills will increase a person's credit score and show creditors that the person is financially responsible. A pattern of repeated late payments will lower a person's score. Infrequent late payments over a long period of time will not ruin a credit score.

People sometimes find it necessary to carry a balance on their credit cards. A balance means that the person did not pay a bill's entire amount due. Most credit cards require a minimum payment each month, even if the cardholder wants to carry a balance. The credit card company may report the payment as past due if the cardholder does not pay the minimum amount. It may also charge a late fee when a cardholder fails to pay the minimum amount.

Consumers should keep their overall debt level low. Lenders may be concerned if a person asks for credit while he or she still owes a relatively large amount of money to other

Setting a monthly budget—and sticking to it—will help you avoid getting too deeply into debt and, as a result, maintain a healthy credit score.

lenders. A high level of debt also affects a person's ability to repay loans. A person's income may not stretch far enough to pay for necessities and credit card bills. The longer a person carries debt, the more credit costs.

Efforts to develop and create a good credit score will also help a person manage personal finances effectively. Personal financial advisers give their clients several tips on how to avoid becoming overburdened by debt. They advise people to make a budget. A budget helps a person compare monthly income with the amount needed each month to pay for rent, utilities, food, and other necessities. The remainder is how much money the person has left over each month for savings and optional spending.

No one should spend more than he or she can afford. Before making a purchase, a person should consider how it will affect his or her budget. Credit allows a person to make smart financial decisions. Buying a house, a car, or other major items is a good financial move for many people. Using a credit card makes financial transactions easier and provides cardholders with a range of benefits and rewards. Credit also tempts people into making poor financial decisions. By taking charge of their finances, people can use credit without getting too deeply in debt.

collateral Property that a borrower pledges to protect the interests of a lender.

consumer finance loan A subprime loan typically used to buy cars or make other purchases.

contract A legally enforceable agreement.

credit card balance The amount of money owed to a credit card company.

credit limit The maximum amount of money a credit card company allows a cardholder to charge on a single card.

credit risk The likelihood that a person will repay a loan or other credit obligation.

default A failure to make an on-time payment or a minimum payment on a loan or other credit obligation.

equilibrium The point at which suppliers produce exactly the number of items that consumers want at a specific price.

inflation An increase in prices that reduces the value of money.

installment loan A debt, such as a mortgage, that a borrower pays back in equal payments at regular intervals over time.

monetary policy Changes to the supply of money, or its cost, that a government makes to influence the expansion or contraction of a national economy.

mortgage A long-term loan used to finance the purchase of a house or other property.

prime rate A bank's lowest interest rate, which it offers to its best customers.

reserves Money deposits that a bank keeps in its vaults instead of using to fund loans.

revolving credit A credit account, such as a credit card account, in which a debtor repeatedly borrows and pays back money without reapplying for credit.

subprime rate An interest rate that is higher than a bank's prime rate.

supply and demand The interaction between how much suppliers want to produce at specific prices and how much consumers want to buy at specific prices.

Treasury bill A short-term debt certificate issued by the U.S. Treasury to raise money for the federal government.

Treasury bond A type of long-term debt certificate issued by the U.S. Treasury to raise money for the federal government.

FOR MORE INFORMATION

American Bankers Association
1120 Connecticut Avenue NW
Washington, DC 20036
(800) BANKERS (226-5377)
Web site: http://www.aba.com
The American Bankers Association provides in-depth
information on the U.S. credit and banking systems.

AnnualCreditReport.com
P.O. Box 105283
Atlanta, GA 30348-5283
Web site: http://www.annualcreditreport.com
Created by the three major credit reporting companies,
AnnualCreditReport.com provides consumers in-depth
information on the credit reporting system.

Board of Governors of the Federal Reserve System
20th Street and Constitution Avenue NW
Washington, DC 20551
Web site: http://federalreserve.gov
(800) 337-0429
The Federal Reserve provides many educational resources,
including information on the banking system, interest
rates, and how the organization helps stabilize the
national economy.

Canadian Bankers Association
199 Bay Street, 30th Floor

Toronto, ON M5L 1G2
Canada
(416) 362-6093
Web site: http://www.cba.ca
The Canadian Bankers Association provides information on
interest rates and other Canadian banking topics.

Council for Economic Education
122 East 42nd Street, Suite 2600
New York, NY 10168
(800) 338-1192
Web Site: http://www.councilforeconed.org
The Council for Economic Education provides information
on understanding economics and personal finance.

Federal Trade Commission
600 Pennsylvania Avenue NW
Washington, DC 20580
(202) 326-2222
Web site: http://www.ftc.gov
The Federal Trade Commission provides information on
consumer rights and the laws governing credit cards
and loans.

Junior Achievement USA
One Education Way
Colorado Springs, CO 80906

(719) 540 8000

Web site: http://www.ja.org

Junior Achievement USA provides an annual survey on
teens and personal finance.

Office of Consumer Affairs

Industry Canada

235 Queen Street, 2nd Floor, West Tower

Ottawa, ON K1A 0H5

Canada

(613) 946-2576

Web site: http://www.ic.gc.ca/consumer

Industry Canada's Office of Consumer Affairs provides
information on many credit topics, including credit
reports and how to manage debt.

U.S. Department of Education

400 Maryland Avenue SW

Washington, DC 20202

(800) 872-5327

Web site: http://www.ed.gov

The U.S. Department of Education provides information
about federal student loan programs.

Washington State Department of Financial Institutions

P.O. Box 41200

Olympia, WA 98504-1200

(360) 902-8700

Web site: http://www.dfi.wa.gov/consumers

The Washington State Department of Financial Institutions provides information and free publications on mortgages, payday loans, and other types of credit.

Web Sites

Due to the changing nature of Internet links, Rosen Publishing has developed an online list of Web sites related to the subject of this book. This site is updated regularly. Please use this link to access the list:

http://www.rosenlinks.com/yef/credit

FOR FURTHER READING

Allman, Barbara. *Banking*. Minneapolis, MN: Lerner, 2005.

Bellenir, Karen, ed. *Debt Information for Teens*. Detroit, MI: Omnigraphics, 2008.

Brezina, Corona. *Understanding the Federal Reserve and Monetary Policy*. New York, NY: Rosen Publishing, 2012.

Bryfonski, Dedria. *Student Loans*. San Diego, CA: Greenhaven Press, 2011.

Butler, Tamsen. *The Complete Guide to Personal Finance: For Teenagers and College Students*. Ocala, FL: Atlantic Publishing Group, 2010.

Byers, Ann. *First Credit Cards and Credit Smarts*. New York, NY: Rosen Publishing, 2009.

Challen, Paul, and Jeri S. Cipriano. *How Do Mortgages, Loans, and Credit Work?* New York, NY: Crabtree Publishing, 2009.

Connolly, Sean. *Banks and Banking*. New York, NY: Franklin Watts, 2011.

Deering, Kathryn R., ed. *Cash and Credit Information for Teens*. Detroit, MI: Omnigraphics, 2005.

Espejo, Roman. *Teens and Credit*. San Diego, CA: Greenhaven Press, 2009.

Hall, Alvin. *Show Me the Money: How to Make Cents of Economics*. New York, NY: Dorling Kindersley, 2008.

Hollander, Barbara Gottfried. *How Credit Crises Happen*. New York, NY: Rosen Publishing, 2010.

Hynson, Colin. *The Credit Crunch*. North Mankato, MN: Sea-to-Sea Publications, 2010.

Lawless, Robert E. *The Student's Guide to Financial Literacy*. Santa Barbara, CA: Greenwood Press, 2010.

Macht, Norman. *Money and Banking*. Philadelphia, PA: Chelsea House, 2001.

McCrary, J. *My Money & Me: Managing Money & Credit*. Redondo Beach, CA: Westcom Press, 2010.

Merino, Nicole. *The World Economy*. San Diego, CA: Greenhaven Press, 2010.

Miller, Debra A. *The U.S. Economy*. San Diego, CA: Greenhaven Press, 2010.

Minden, Cecilia. *Using Credit Wisely*. Ann Arbor. MI: Cherry Lake, 2007.

Thompson, Helen. *Understanding Credit*. Broomall, PA: Mason Crest, 2009.

BIBLIOGRAPHY

Board of Governors of the Federal Reserve. "A Consumer's Guide to Mortgage Refinancing." Retrieved March 12, 2009 (http://www.federalreserve.gov/pubs /refinancings/default.htm).

Board of Governors of the Federal Reserve. "Credit Reports and Credit Scores." Retrieved March 12, 2012 (http:// www.federalreserve.gov/creditreports).

Board of Governors of the Federal Reserve. "Purposes and Functions." Retrieved March 12, 2012 (http://www .federalreserve.gov/pf/pdf/pf_complete.pdf).

Canadian Consumer Handbook. "Mortgages." Retrieved March 12, 2012 (http://www.consumerhandbook.ca /en/topics/financial/mortgages).

Federal Trade Commission. "Building a Better Credit Report." Retrieved March 12, 2012 (http://www.ftc.gov /bcp/edu/pubs/consumer/credit/cre03.shtm).

Federal Trade Commission. "Credit and Your Consumer Rights." Retrieved March 12, 2012 (http://www.ftc.gov /bcp/edu/pubs/consumer/credit/cre01.shtm).

Federal Trade Commission. "Equal Credit Opportunity: Understanding Your Rights Under the Law." Retrieved March 12, 2009 (http://www.ftc.gov/bcp/edu/pubs /consumer/credit/cre15.shtm).

Federal Trade Commission. "Getting Credit." Retrieved March 12, 2009 (http://www.ftc.gov/bcp/conline /edcams/gettingcredit).

Federal Trade Commission. "Getting Credit: What You Need to Know About Credit." Retrieved March 12, 2012

(http://www.ftc.gov/bcp/edu/pubs/consumer/credit
/cre32.shtm).

Federal Trade Commission. "Need Credit or Insurance? Your
Credit Score Helps Determine What You'll Pay."
Retrieved March 12, 2012 (http://www.ftc.gov/bcp
/edu/pubs/consumer/credit/cre24.shtm).

Federal Trade Commission. "Understanding Vehicle
Financing." Retrieved March 12, 2012 (http://www.ftc
.gov/bcp/edu/pubs/consumer/autos/aut04.shtm).

Mankiw, N. Gregory. *Essentials of Economics*. Mason, OH:
Cengage Learning, 2011.

Mankiw, N. Gregory. *Principles of Economics*. Mason, OH:
Cengage Learning, 2011.

MyFICO.com. "About Credit Scores." Retrieved March 12,
2012 (http://www.myfico.com/crediteducation
/creditscores.aspx).

MyFICO.com. "What's in Your FICO Score." Retrieved March
12, 2012 (http://www.myfico.com/crediteducation
/whatsinyourscore.aspx).

Rosefsky, Robert. *Personal Finance*. New York, NY: Wiley,
2002.

Sowell, Thomas. *Basic Economics*. 4th ed. New York, NY:
Basic Books, 2010.

U.S. Department of Education. "Direct Loans." Retrieved
March 12, 2012 (http://www.direct.ed.gov).

Weston, Liz Pulliam. *Your Credit Score*. Upper Saddle River,
NJ: FT Press, 2009.

A

accounts, checking, 33
agencies, credit reporting, 6, 52–53, 63

B

background checks, 61
banking, how it works, 33–36
bonds, 13, 28, 50–51
budget, personal, 66
budget deficit, 26
budget surplus, 26

C

car loans, 6, 8, 17, 24, 35, 38, 41
checking accounts, 33
checks, background, 61
collateral, 35–36
credit
  and businesses, 13, 21, 24
  and government, 13, 21, 24
  and supply and demand, 21–23, 24, 40
credit cards, 6, 9–11, 12, 13, 16, 53, 54, 55, 56, 59, 60, 64–65, 66

credit history and scores, 54
  and employers, 52, 59, 61–64
  establishing good, 54, 64–66
  and landlords, 52, 59, 64
  and loans, 6, 35, 38, 53–58, 59–61
credit line, 14
credit reporting agencies, 6, 52–53, 63

D

dealership financing, 38
debit cards, 35
debt, good as compared to bad, 14–16
deficit, budget, 26
demand, 17–21
  and credit, 21–23
Direct Loan Program, 39
discount rate, 29

E

education loans, 6, 15, 38–39
equilibrium, 20

F

Fair Credit Reporting
Act, 63
Federal Family Education
Loan Program, 39
Federal Reserve, 26–29, 48
Federal Trade Commission, 16
FICO score, 53–58
finance charge, 17, 32, 38

I

inflation, 24–25, 31, 48
interbank rate, 29, 31, 48
interest, 5, 7, 13, 15, 16, 17,
21–26, 32, 33, 36, 38,
40, 43, 50–51, 57
and the economy, 12, 28–31,
42, 44–48

J

J.D. Power and Associates, 8

L

landlords, 52, 59, 64
loans, 8, 9, 11, 12, 13, 14,
15, 16, 17, 24–25,
28–29, 35, 44–46

and credit scores, 5–7,
40–41, 53–58, 59–61
mechanics of, 32
types of, 36–39

M

mortgages, 5–7, 16, 17,
24, 35, 36–38, 41,
43, 44–46, 52, 58

O

online shopping, 12

P

payday loans, 16
Perkins loans, 38
personal budget, 66
prime rate, 41
principal, 32, 36

R

risk, 40–41

S

savings, 21–23, 28, 33, 35, 50
security deposits, 64

Social Security, 23
Stafford loans, 39
subprime rates, 41, 57, 58
supply, 17–21
 and credit, 21–23
surplus, budget, 26

T

taxes, 25–26, 50
TransUnion, 52, 53

U

U.S. Department of
 Education, 39
U.S. Treasury, 13, 28

V

VantageScore, 53, 58

About the Author

G. S. Prentzas has written more than two dozen books for young readers. He writes articles on personal finance, business, law, and other topics for Chron.com, LegalZoom.com, and other Web sites. He graduated from the University of North Carolina with an A.B. with honors in English (economics double major) and a J.D. with honors.

Photo Credits

Cover (bottom) © iStockphoto.com/Gaja Snover; cover (ragged paper) © iStockphoto.com/Petek Arici; pp. 4–5, 60–61 Image Source/Getty Images; pp. 8, 17, 32, 42, 52, 59 © iStockphoto.com/Ivan Bliznetsov; pp. 10–11 Digital Vision/ Thinkstock; p. 13 Vladimir Godnik/the Agency Collection/ Getty Images; pp. 15, 40–41 Comstock/Thinkstock; pp. 18–19, 36–37 © AP Images; pp. 22–23 John-Francis Bourke/The Image Bank/Getty Images; pp. 26–27 Mladen Antonov/AFP/Getty Images; p. 30 Chip Somodevilla/Getty Images; pp. 34–35 Bloomberg/Getty Images; p. 39 Courtesy of Edvisors Network, Inc.; pp. 44–45 Justin Sullivan/Getty Images; pp. 46–47 Laura Gangi Pond/Shutterstock.com; pp. 48–49 Spencer Platt/Getty Images; p. 55 Courtesy of Equifax, Inc.; p. 56 Copyright © FICO. Used with permission. FICO, myFICO, the FICO logo, and the FICO product and service names are trademarks or registered trademarks of FICO; p. 62 © iStockphoto.com/Amanda Rohde; p. 65 Avava/Shutterstock.com.

Designer: Michael Moy; Editor: Nicholas Croce;
Photo Researcher: Marty Levick